Poems by Nance Van Winckel

Bad Girl, with Hawk

University of Illinois Press   *Urbana and Chicago*

Publication of this work was supported in part by grants from the National Endowment for the Arts and the Illinois Arts Council, a state agency.

© 1988 by Nance Van Winckel
Manufactured in the United States of America
P 5 4 3 2 1

This book is printed on acid-free paper.

Thanks to the editors of the following publications in which these poems first appeared:

"Bad Girl, with Hawk," in *The American Poetry Review.*
"Counting Toward Sleep" and "Goodnight," in *Poetry.*
"Change of Heart," "The Trainmaster's Thunder," "Deserting the Town," "Lost in Riverview Trailer Court," "First Things, Last Things," "Coming Home from the Big Game," "Children Too Near the Freeway," "The Many Beds of Martha Washington," and "She Who Hunts," in various issues of *Poetry Northwest.*
"American Promises," in *Poetry Now.*
"Holding Together," in *The Denver Quarterly.*
"Just Be Home Before Sundown," "Apology," "All He Asks," "House of Clues," and "Basket with Blue Ox," in *The Iowa Review.*
"You Get So," in *The Georgia Review.*

Library of Congress Cataloging-in-Publication Data

Van Winckel, Nance.
  Bad girl, with hawk : poems / by Nance Van Winckel.
    p. cm.
  ISBN 0-252-01503-7 (pbk. : alk. paper)
  I. Title.
PS3572.A546B3 1988
811'.54—dc19   87-24483
                                                    CIP

for Rik

CONTENTS

From this the poem springs: that we live in a place
That is not our own and, much more, not ourselves
And hard it is in spite of blazoned days.

—Stevens, "Notes Toward a Supreme Fiction"

I

But I shrug off the red sweater
she's knit around me. It's not in me
to keep my shoulders always warm.
Or to get off the bus every time
at our same spot, as if other
squared-off corners were not so splendid.
Besides, I've seen what's going up
down the block: a village of workers
moving in behind a facade of little doors,
and on the block beyond that, a steel ball
sending the bricks of an old building
everywhere. Besides, I keep asking, *Which
sun do you mean?* She just answers
something about my father. What can he do
that takes all day? His shoulders
go out into light and bring back dusk
as far as the doorstep. I've seen his maps
crumpled on the car seat, his inked lines
wavering across the corn belt, which he says
strangled the breath last year
out of all of us. Besides, I can't listen
any more to the supper music—violins
skipping their best notes in the scarred
grooves of slow-falling twilight
in the edges of the room I want only
to be out of, out amid the jazz
of crickets, my mouth filled
with the firm gristle of night,
the pop and fizz of traffic,
headlights and dark roads colliding.

APOLOGY

The sick watercolor ducks
on the wall would also be gone
if they had some place to go,
if they had not lost themselves
in too much too blue sky.
My bathwater turning colder,
I watch them and complain.
Mother pours another hot potful in.
What poverty can this be? Food
and wood enough for winter,
maples turning everywhere
in the yard of an uncle's summer
cottage. I am still too young
to understand. Grandmother puts on
another sweater, bangs another pot
onto its hook, says she knew
any deal like that
would end like this.
Beside my big round tub
mother's words mist and lift
into the cool air I must soon
reenter. But for now I am no one.
Barely six. Tomorrow I'll say
my vowels finally right. And tomorrow,
my sister is sure, even the cold water pipes
will freeze. I sink deeper,
making the room go quiet.
Just my eyes and the top of my head
bob on the edge
of an incredibly warm world.
Across the kitchen women's shadows
drift, their breaths barely seen,
gone. And then father and his shadow
step forward, and behind him

the little clouds of his words,
so familiar—one, then
the other—I'm sorry.

COUSINS

Something's circling inside him,
the doctor told us, that makes his eyes
go back, his legs go out. That was one
cousin. He fell on the steps. He fell
in the disked field. There were two more
like him. They'd go down and after a while
get up and brush the dirt off.

Way back there was an uncle, and once
he'd had a choice and done the wrong
thing. An old woman in town said this.
She wouldn't say what the right thing was.

When they came to our house
my sister and I whispered about crows
fluttering up and down the thin stalks
of their spines. One cousin stayed inside
to rest on a sofa, while the other two
stood with us in the yard where the frogs
were early and full of singing.

That's when another one went down.
A moment before he had been standing
as well as anyone. He'd said the names
of some little families of stars.
My sister and I stopped whispering
and looked up. The other cousin
had known what to do. They were down there
a long time on the wet grass.
Then a few more stars came out. And those frogs,
they didn't know to shut up.

Long summers we hid in the rubble
of an old pool, or in a heap of lumber
where a large house collapsed.
We searched until there was no one
to find—you and I the last

to disappear over the edge
of our steep embankment, down there
where the highway sent out its loud roar.
Shimmering on the far lane—new tar
so black it was blue. We'd heard

of the call of catastrophe,
how soon enough we'd go everywhere.
In both directions at once cars
hurtled themselves toward what
pitiful places we could barely imagine.

From the ledge we could feel each one
pass us, a hot gust through the face.
We could see each end of the road, like two
ends of a rope, stop—the cars cut loose
into separate invisible space.

Bloated with heat, the afternoons
moved us slowly. Except for the time
I could not move: kicking over an old brick,
I sent six young moccasins rushing past my ankles
and in the one painful breath I could breathe

I called your name. But then
the traffic sounds, carried up
on a sudden wind, were so loud
I couldn't find your voice
coming back for me: *I'm here, I'm here.*

WALKING GRANDFATHER HOME

The terms of our deal were never said —
not to say where he'd been, where
I'd been. Late afternoons I'd stop off
to get him, though maybe he happened to be
in the bar where some boy I was after
shot pool in a swarm of smoke.
The old men, farmers, filled the air
with the dull mysteries of weather
and rifts of unanswerable accusations:
stolen calves, rifles, women.

Farther in, I followed a face that stayed
in shadow. His cue said everything
between us. Already I'd learned to laugh
my serious laugh. Light from the door
through the men's mugs punctured our dark path
with small gold globes. I was sure
the angle of a perfect shot was more
than luck, something honest as science.
And sure nothing he'd done could be as bad
as the way voices fell upon the stories.

The sound I listened for was grandfather's
empty glass on the bar. He wouldn't wait,
not even a minute. And walking home
on the dusky sidewalks, his conversations —
the curiosities of love or crime — seemed as much
with himself as with me. Except for trees.
When he spoke of them I looked up. I spoke too —
of how they bend lower in autumn as night
begins, the new longer night, the one
that still leaves its residue of questions.

COMING HOME FROM THE BIG GAME

For sixteen miles we've reviewed strategies,
the rush of bodies up the field and back,
honored our debt to the chalked little X's
and O's, and to the strange disguises
worn for a last time to please us.

The bottle passes between us, more delicious
than the blurred words that follow it
around the bus, which keeps dragging us
farther up this unfamiliar road
into the mountain's cold blue shadow.

We've beat our hands like tiny drums
all evening until only darkness
covered the flattened grass. But now we clap
for what is about to be memory — until
the thud of death makes a hole in our story.

Our hands pause in the air as if startled
from an embrace. Then we're climbing down
from the warmth of close bodies onto the black
highway — a circle of teenagers finally silent
under the slightest possible moon. And there

half under our wheels, half out, is the long
dark creature who saw our beautiful lights
and stepped forward to meet us. We breathe together
among those last hard breaths,
breathe in the blame, all of it.

BAD GIRL, WITH HAWK

The hawk, a smudge on the sky, cuts a swath
across a field where men repeat themselves
with a stutter that goes on all day: Bend
and pick. Bend and pick. Little green pods
stack up on their backs. The hawk had nowhere
to go. I watched him from the road, knowing
there was somewhere I should have been, still

more conjugations I should be saying, the Spanish
romper, to tear, though I'd ripped the heart
out of the language of backseats, the old
Plymouth with its mouth deep enough that a boy
might follow a girl into it, as if no road
up the mountain could not be outlived:
Land of huge nests for huge, wonderful birds.

Only the lab lights shone down a few bright hours.
I pulled the starfish apart, left its splendid body
to limp home across the tank. Some days even I did
as I was told: a lost angel who had yet to know
grace, though I'd seen it in the hawk's flight down
over a thousand small bodies littering the field
and toward the single mole that was its target.

But a child lived near me, and once I tried
too hard to push her out of thunder and hail.
Then came the white jolt that tore her stroller
from my hand and rolled it into her mother's
rock garden: First the tooth through her lip,
next the scar she would always pin by my name,
and then my last late arrival to the table

around which sat my family of little red rocks,
the bowl of green peas circling, as if somehow
everything had been settled, as if finally each
white mind behind those four sets of blue eyes
knew me. My evil days were numbered. The peas
stopped by my plate. I lifted my spoon. And then
the hymns of forgiveness began, my undoing.

AUTUMN NOSTALGIA

All the streets through town were hung
with the carcasses of deer. On every porch
two pairs of hooves were roped
to the rafters. And to a stranger
approaching at nightfall, a deer
swaying there could resemble a dark
hammock, one that he might crawl into
and dream off the whole of autumn,
while venison smoke thickened to a cloud,
rose, and settled on the rooftops.

And driving Hwy. 50, I recognize that cloud
dragging the outskirts like a loose hem.
All afternoon I've rushed past the blue bins
and baffling red barns of my girlhood.
What lives there, old men used to say,
is a winter of food for a good country.

At the edge of town smoke falters
among stands of trees, unable to tear itself
away. I drive through that cloud,
letting its sweet musk sweep me
along streets where nothing has changed—
the little brick stores that sold me
the goods of my life. The swaying carcasses

make even the sidewalks appear to sway—
to and from these streets, where during one
absolute end of Indian summer
I walked through rain-clogged gutters.
Storm clouds broke open above me.
I was wet to the bone,

so wet I stepped into the drugstore
and stood like a stranger by the door.
Though the bell tinkled, no one
looked up. Barefoot, I made a quick orbit
through the aisles. There was nothing
I could think to need. Then I made
the bell go off again, and I looked back
through the huge window at the wet prints
of my feet, that one crooked toe.

II

PATRONYMIC

Two thousand miles west and I'm back
among my family of bad bones, back
walking out through the bare evening,
only their old name draped on my shoulders.

I shake loose my legs from their aches
and run. Familiar lights gather
in my back's shadow where they do
little good. I turn corners, my feet

finding footholds in the dark. Beyond
my life this name has nowhere to go now,
no sons to visit itself upon — just me,
the daughter who'll drag it again

across a wide continent, or what's worse,
through her small, irregular heart.
My steps drop their echoes behind,
as I run through this night

which is the one night that pulls us
around, and so, tumbles us smooth.
I run up it and down it, the one night
that slips forward, over, down.

HOLDING TOGETHER

Outside, our narrow sky darkens, pulls in.
We grow lean and remark on the shrinking shadows
of our brothers, the small elms.

Near dusk we watch the swift drop
beyond us, to the rooftop. She pants, waiting,
we suppose, for disaster from the sky.

And in the pond our old friend the fish —
whose tail fin long ago snapped off —
he treads water, watches

for opportunities. And when they come,
cautionless, he envelopes them
with the long horizon of his body.

Soon we hear father's step on the lawn.
At his side he carries his new steel elbow,
marveling at its cool absence of pain.

Now there are three of us, two sisters
and an old man. And even in this delicate breeze
we seem unsteady, a line of loose limbs

trying to stand themselves up
with no help, but for the wild yellow hair
that spreads out above them, feeling for light.

LISTENING TO THE CHILDREN
PLAY MOZART

We sit high up in the tall balconies
and watch the children we should have been
play music. They wear bangled blindfolds
and smile. Handfuls of copper pennies
fly around them in the colorful air.

Later we'll languish in the arias of these
memories, in the operatic constructs
of their locked catwalks.
And so our city fills with music,
is hung high and wide

with longing's unfulfillable notes,
vague melodies that come and go
as shadows of something we almost
recognize: we look back up the block,
abstracted, unclear. Like children

we cast our lot to this town
and come in from its streets
with clear needs: we want back
the music we played once,
warm days of deep notes
into which we pressed our echoes
and made them stay.

HOUSE OF CLUES

After dinner there are board games
on the floor. Our hands push
the tin pipes, the knives
and crowbars, in one room and out
another. Although not a part
of the game, we reward ourselves
with money. How well we know
each other—faces, hands—the lucent
images that fill memory
with what fingertips have felt,
memory that lies like some larger
board between us,

large enough for a thousand rooms.
We roam them easily, though unsure
of a single door. Here
we enter, and here leave,
all of us at once—now in our young
bodies, now in our old. We step
into bedrooms and kitchens and call
each others' names into the dim light.

Finally it is my turn to drag
a heavy thing into the library
where the odor of death is a little nudge
of *deja vu.* Is it not inevitable
that I must open my heart, that friends
will stumble over one
or another of my many crimes?

I may as well turn up my cards,
those vengeful faces I've held too long.
Let them be taken, shuffled
together with the others, as if truth
puts an end to such play, as if at last
we might walk out of this busy house.

AND NOW, MORE RAIN

I am not what you think.
I am not the fireman approaching
your door in his rowboat—there
to take your barking dog
and your grandfather's fiddle.

Nor am I the voice of your neighbor
who swims over, dragging his big bucket,
his pumps and hoses. More
rubber rafts drift into your yard

but I am not in one. And I
am certainly not the sunlight
breaking free and settling like the soft wisps
of a young girl's hair on your shoulder.
This will not happen for days

no matter what we sell of ourselves,
no matter what we curse or bless to make it
happen. I am the bank the river
rises above, the long stretch
of washed-out road, and the gash
ripping deeper into the storm cloud. I am part
of the sadness of unstoppable water.

GIRL WITH ONE ARM DOWN
THE ZUPECK STREET DRAIN

I can't imagine what
she wants so badly
to bring up and out
from the lost world.
Only her child's hand
could find a path
through the metal grate;
only that slimmest of arms
could push a way clear
through the sediment
of mud and bad omens.
Soon she's turned
sideways, facing me
across the street, letting
her arm and precious hand
do this thing for her, alone
and beyond sight.

A little group who may
be her friends, or almost
friends, watch from a porch
three houses down. All
they can see is her head, bent
to its single task, held
to the spot where grey streets
face each other down. Too
busy to see the friends, or me,
she pulls the arm out
and pushes it back again
as if this were her last chance
to bring forth a small good thing
to our neighborhood, whose luck
must be about to change.

BASKET WITH BLUE OX

for Donna

Today it seems plausible that myth alone could
have made this place, or made it possible
at least for us to be here, this small lake
where once the great woodsman stepped,
drunkenly, on his way home. Cross-legged
on the dock we weave baskets of willow,
mulberry root, small nests we dip again
and again into the cool water. Only here
could everything the past imagined for us
seem true: how spring is a single season,
that it somehow makes us tender. Or that
the blue ox lies down each night on the far
shore and wakes with a breath that blows off
morning's fog. In their unsinkable boats
our husbands fish close to that shore
as we continue these baskets, fill them
with stories. Our friend the loon listens
to tale after tale; his cries of belief detonate
on the still air. Today the preposterous lies
line up in our baskets on the dock.
We have made them and there is no limit
to what they can hold. The lake is nothing less
than the footprint of a man, these baskets the honor
of hopeful hands, and men in boats must come back,
ushering in the dark, carrying beautiful fishes.

24

COUNTING TOWARD SLEEP

From each corner the grey cranes appear
and, as if wingless, march off like old
soldiers, rifle-beaks bobbing up the walls
high into the blue shadows of sleep.

I count the sadnesses of their leaving.
Beneath each of us the earth's deep fires
breathe in, burning brighter with every sudden
rift, every little addition of gritty fuel.

And now I sink down upon it all: the fallen birds,
our warm pallet of earth. And soon the stream
lies down through me. Rattling and spewing, it sends
rocks tumbling. Wild lilies break loose, travel.

There is too much everywhere
not to observe.
Far into morning, sheep
on every finger — Dorsetts
and Corriedales — my hand
is a meadow.

III

1

I keep an eye on the trailers
and think of smooth cylinders
flattened against huge trees,
knocked into four dull edges.

There is a song to go with such
beatings. It is one Tsai Lun sang
making his origami puzzles.
I'm singing it now, trying to piece
together the sound of these insects
and the steady slap of the river.

And here, that house. Made of map
paper. I try to read the walls.
The polar rings sit sideways,
humming along. Here there is no mistake.
I've gotten my directions confused.
Lost, lost again.

From their small yards old women nod.
Boys peer out from beneath wrecked cars.

A taxi or a patrol car
could never find me here
without an address: every number
and street sign camouflaged
in some obscene calligraphy.

This must be the time I've known
was coming. I fold in my legs, make a lotus.
Concentration. Control. Begin again.
I find a soggy direction book, read:
Crawl through side A onto floor B.

Straddle beam 12. Cross
to door P. Someone else is humming.
Soon the whole trailer court has joined in
as if they know the chorus.

I make the correct gash in section C.
Turn page. I read the small print:
It's not much, but you can make it home.
Repeat steps 2 and 3.

2

I sit on the curb to think
through these new developments.
All around the squared tubes sit quietly.
But behind those onion-skinned windows
the fat necks turn and turn.
They wonder about my next move.

A corner trailer looks empty
and behind my left eye a new plan
has begun to take hold. I cross carefully
like a desperate woman. I slide my hand
over the cardboard walls, crawl up
on the roof to check for leaks.
Finally I go under, easing my spine
down against the damp earth, sliding
like a long wet animal beneath the floor.

Soon I find I am moving like my old self:
unloading my car and arranging my possessions.
Drinking the water. Flushing the toilet.
Making sure the phone is disconnected.

3

I am learning to disregard the peripheral fear
of the scarred white edges of my neighbors' faces
and the quick sounds of their metal blades in the night.

From my own tattered box I hike farther
and farther toward the inner court. This is how
I have made my wonderful discoveries.
Everywhere, like young cactuses they open
their pink blossoms: so small and lovely
and tortuous. One, a boy on his bicycle,
realizes he can fly. He comes shooting out
from the origami maze with the words still wet
on his lips. *I'm flying. I'm flying.*
His wheels spin at waist level.

The young girl by the river—she too is a wonder.
She has had her vision: Riverview disappearing
inside the long blue funnel of a tornado
while she rises from the top like a goddess
and floats out beyond the ionosphere.
I could come with her, she suggests,
picturing herself landing gracefully
in some antiseptic interstellar city.
But I shake my head. Mosquitoes buzz.
Riverview sparkles around us like an emerald,
flat and miraculously close to the ground.
I write my name on the thin walls, saying,
I have already landed here.

SINK OR SWIM

When he's released from his father's hands
too much air unbalances him. Then rage,
like gravity, lets go too, lets him go
nowhere but down. Into waters reeling

with the fluid faces of drowned boys
that the clumsy oars of his body must pull
steadily through. And finally loosed
from the leash of his father's eyes,

from even the shadows of those eyes
dispersing through the dense cold,
he touches new land. Bright pebbles
rouse themselves a little, as if he'd been

expected—sooner or later. As if life
could only resume itself this way—
in a cold, deep place, breathless, the body
thrashing toward elusive tunnels of air.

FIRST THINGS, LAST THINGS

1

A young woman falls backward
into sleep. In her arms her doll,
its china head just split
by a stone. Fallen. And even before that
the arc of the stone, its long curve
over peonies, over the child
she was then
crouched over tiny tea cups.

And before that
the cruel curve of the neighbor boy's
dark arm lifting, almost
as if to greet her, the palm
opening, the rock flying, falling,
finding its way — this long
and this hard — toward hurt.

2

White sun. White fever. Hung up
in the shadows and leaves, she swings.
She never tires of what rises
and falls like a rhyme,
warm hands against her back keeping time,
white sun hammering the ground,
white feet hammering the sky
into which she can never fall.

3

Along their road men her father hired
dig a ditch, a ditch for rain

to roll itself away in. She is seven.
For days she watches the picks lift
into a haze of heat. August. Dark sweat
rolling like rain down dark backs.
And one afternoon she sees a man lie down
in the ditch. She sees the new-turned dirt
roll over him like a wave. Then the others
stop, their duty shaken. Every shovel
and pick fall down. How long did she
stand there at the window, whispering
oh please get up, oh please, oh please. . . .

4

Only years away from the present
she is only moments away from the man
who climbed a tower in the center of town.
So high, his head a small pink cloud,
he raised a bullhorn and a rifle,
said he'd come to deliver the suffering ants
who had gone suddenly crazy below.
And he released them. He let them go and go.

5

She wakes with the murmur of suffering
she keeps close to her heart. And almost
as close—the little white cures she keeps
on the bedside table. All night just an arm's
reach across the space of dreams. All night
as the lights click off down the block
the sufferings and the cures go on rising
and falling through the dark together.

YELLOW: COMING AND GOING

A man comes up from his manhole
in the middle of the intersection downtown

to put on his yellow rain slicker. For days
we have been maneuvering around him. Saws

and sawed-off pipes rise up from his hole
while we wait for lights to change.

Now he's taking his time snapping
the snaps, the way he takes his time

down there where something must be
dreadfully wrong. He lifts his hood,

lights a cigarette, and watches the rain
which seems to fall like nobody's business.

Then here comes the yellow schoolbus
hurrying through a yellow light.

It swerves around his hole. The backs
of the children lean hard to the right,

then to the left in a graceful allowance
they gladly give to him, this man

who's finally made up his mind
to go back down there.

In thunderstorms he imagines himself
a good father, going downstairs
to calm the children.
From the top step
he watches them pour cold tea
into tiny china cups.
Like perfect hosts, they nod
and whisper to each other
across a low table.
Then, going back up,
he turns briefly to see
only their small round heads
at the center of a marble floor.

Up there in his room he fabricates
volcano smoke in a metal box.
Hunched and stiff, he sits
under the thin wooden platform of his world.
He flips switches, adjusts the dials.
Above him, at one edge of his landscape
is the cardboard mountain range
where soon the volcano will erupt,
and at the opposite edge
something like an ocean
beats at a sandpaper shore.

Down there under the tracks he listens
to the steady whir of trains going
round and round. Suddenly, outside his window
a long arm of electric light breaks—
the perfect sound effect. He counts,
One-one-thousand, two-one-thousand, . . .
and waits for the next one,

trying to synchronize it
with the coming eruption.

Then the crack of the bone
of light, and how sad, he thinks,
always having to sit down here
making everything happen
when all he ever wanted
was to watch.

AMERICAN PROMISES

Beside the river
a boy, almost twenty,
feeds the ducks
under a steel bridge
and thinks about a girl
he loves

or could love
all night under
a different sort of bridge,

so he feels nothing
when the ducks
mistake his hand
for a small stale loaf.

Far behind his eyes
she has begun undressing,
her body, pale and thin,
already sinking deeper
into the wet brown clay.

And when the real crumbs
are finally gone
he climbs back up the slick bank,
realizing at once
the blood at his fingertips
and the March rain
just beginning to fall.

CHANGE OF HEART

Pausing before the blue shoes,
in mid-zip of the blue dress,
she reconsiders, wants back
last night's every word.

Outside, a confusion of chickory
and cornflowers blows sunlight
to pieces, and morning seems unsure
of the right place to light.

Changing into the yellow dress,
finally she's ready to believe love
just an understandable mistake
of the hands: their sad geometries,

the uneven blocks of quilt
they keep rolling back, or how,
lifting off suddenly across a strange
new body, they hesitate, then

fold themselves there in some deep
presumptuous sleep. Tying
and retying the yellow belt,
she remembers a girl who in the heat

of too many clothes began walking
into the river. Behind her,
on the shore, a line of wild singers
had their faces to the sky.

The water felt like nothing.
Farther out, the man who waited
to take her to Jesus raised his arms
higher than arms should be able to go

as she walked past him and on
toward that far bank of quiet
cottonwoods, each one bending down
in the wrong direction.

SHE WHO HUNTS

1

She knows to wait in the thicket, to stoop
ready among its brambles, soundless as snow.

But first, like snow, she must gather herself,

a long inhaling for the long letting go, the breath
given up into freezing air. Slowly the earth,

the earth comes up to meet her. This meeting
the hunters call patience.

2

Hours in the thicket. Legs of thorns.
Briars up her dead calves. Her back
burrowing a nest there, its slow
sinking as she listens for deer, light

careful footsteps. With the surprise
and strength of her quiet, she calls them.

3

Days of snow. The thicket full, deep
around her. Only her eyes, blue blades,
cut through the wide white clearing
where the one who can
no longer resist her vigil
must come forward
and release her.

4

Or not. That no deer remain.
That she will wait for one more new moon
to open, or for the starlight of April alone

to melt her, return her
to her stiff little sac of flesh.
And that the earth will fall away
into mud, deepening rot,
and she in her thicket
with it. All that she considers.

5

Disentangling herself from the brambles,
she shakes off the white mantle and goes to him.
Her hand divides his body, empties him clean.

His eyes, the darker black of many nights
to come, watch as her knife goes down.

And the arrow in her hand again as if it had never
left. The weight of snow is a memory
on her shoulder, and the fear her arm
pulled back, pulled and pulled. How
had she let go? How had she sent
warm blood rushing into the trees?
And how long before she forgets
what she's done here, how she's done it.

IV

DESERTING THE TOWN

Weak from too little blood, I arrive
on the last stagecoach ever to cross
these dirt streets. And when it leaves
all the good folks' faces leave too — hanging
from the doors and windows, watching
their own dust on the rise behind them.

Though I am the first stranger in months,
no one has stayed to share
a sidewalk with me. Or a bottle.
My name must carry too much
with it: the many dead silences
of the many long afternoons, fires shrinking

amid shrinking familial rooms, and out
in the descendent twilight, the barely
perceptible moans of horses dispersing
into the hills. And then the face itself,
its large recognizable lucency, the pale
round thing on them everywhere in the dark.

*　*　*

Beneath these streets the silver has vanished,
the last of a last vein gone dry, one pulse
at a time. The walls of the empty mine shake
themselves. And like an explosion into the past,
my life could drop through anytime, fall
as far back as a mind's eye can travel:

the receding splits and schisms down there
in the narrow tunnels of other people's history
where once there were reasons for vulgar
whiskey, for threats, bad debts, mud and

knives and grease. There were reasons my name
stayed in everyone's mouth like sour milk.

*   *   *

I am tired and cannot travel
beyond the city's easy limits,
though I remember the way night there
scattered itself across the fields of poppies,
day lilies, and wild zinnias, and earth
came to a place where it seemed to stop

and resolve itself in a wall of cerulean
sky. But the streets here do not lead
to that place. The streets here do not
meet under that horizon, but cross in
and back on their bleak little futures
of cave-in upon cave-in.

Hundreds of pages of days later
I sign my name to the guest book
and take the circular stairs
up. Here's the narrow room
with its one straight bed.
Here's the stain where she spilt
her port, lying down alone
on some blustery winter eve.
She undid her corset stays,
pulled the pins from her wig.
When would those well-dressed
skeletons in her closet stop
rattling their loose bones?

*   *   *

First came the recitation of her list,
all the things she'd ask for: two
tall pewter candlesticks, a sketch
of the new capital, white bonnet,
new scullery girl. . . . Next the hum
in the spinning house of the sixteen wheels,
or a plan for new cloth striped
with silk scraps from her old
brown stockings. Nothing could make her
stay alone in that place. At night
from across the Potomac the banished
red man rows his bark boat. He comes
and goes, dragging behind him the spirits
of the Great Forest. He must do this, not
for himself, but for the felled trees,
the misplaced stones, the hewn earth.

*   *   *

Hers was a night's rest on the way
to one last front, one last
icy campaign. What did she think
the shooting was all about: a country
little more than a name, without credit
or power. I climb up the short ladder.

Across the coverlet night's shadows
dispatch the damask figures,
little soldiers joined hand to rifle
to hand. Hurry, hurry, they call
to their real lovers, the breezes waiting
in the eaves. Sleep is a power we're given
but do not possess. Tie the white bonnet
tighter. Bring on the dreams.
In them what's been wronged
is further wronged, or righted.

OUTDOOR MOVIE

Spearfish, South Dakota. 1947.

On the screen Moses lifts his staff, and lightning
rips a hole in the clouds behind him. For years
he has walked his rage through the desert, shouted
to followers across wide distances, his white beard
blown back from the dark cavities of his eyes,

which look out now over the black shining bubbles
of Hudsons and DeSotos, neat rows of them. Inside,
the couples lean forward toward what must happen next:
a sea that undoes itself like a red silk dress. No one
can move. Out beyond the dark side of the screen

the sun has burned its way down, left its bloody trail
across the sheer face of the Black Hills. And just
as the air, cooled by twilight, fills the last
windshield with fog, a man whose robes flail wildly
steps between two tumultuous walls of water.

THANKSGIVING PLAY

The mayor and the orthodontist wheel in
a cart full of pumpkins. All of us
are here in good faith, small souvenirs
for our neighbors' amusement. The good wife
I am, Goody N., makes her entrance, a woman
bereft of any moment's present—neither torment
nor simple tedium. I keep an eye on heaven
and my heart marooned on a heathen shore.

With the others in these simple bonnets,
white and stiff, I whisper and nod approvingly
as the town delinquent walks in the turkey
on its leash. A troubled boy with a musket,
he accepts this duty as if failure
were no longer possible. He says
his two lines with perfect solemnity.

Am I the only player confused by an old
chemistry churning within? Whose prim
little ghost moves and speaks this way,
falls surprised over its own rememberings:
days in the woods, painful autumns, new corn—
that uncertain satisfaction for the hungers of March—
a heavy weapon on the shoulder, the black
powder deep down, thin frost on the pond's
thin ice—such treachery—and nights
in the woods—trees, trees without end.

Seated about our feast table, we bow our heads
over the papier-mâché vegetables, the colorful
gourds. And though the curtain keeps on falling,
we want never to leave our table. We want
to continue this prayer for pumpkins,
more pumpkins—sweeter and fatter.

YOU GET SO

The road gets as far west as the east slope
and gives up. The crew is nothing
but patient, standing aside for the man
who lives to blow things up. *You get so
you can do it,* he says, his pockets full of fuses.

The bosses watch from the air where the road
through the mountain must seem but the slightest
possibility, a straight line only a fine eye
could cut through granite,
through years of determined wind.

The man shouts something to the crew
who back off again. He's tinkering
with a charge, rescrewing a blasting cap.
You get so it doesn't matter. Then a copse
of cedar goes down like a clean strike.

Circling, circling, the bosses wonder
how else to reward him, what's enough
for a man for whom mountains lie down
to let him walk through—the others
following with their little white lights,

pausing here and there to dig at something
that does not yet entirely exist.
You get so it comes easy. The road falls
open, and a few men pass over it
and get a little farther on.

ALL HE ASKS

Nome, Alaska. 1907.

1

The stone carver is looking away
into the dust riding everywhere
on the air around the white man.

And when he touches the green stone,
he cannot feel within it
what the white man has asked:

the sleek caribou, sharp antlers,
quick hooves. Now the stone warms
as if it has always lived
just here in the palm of a man's hand.

2

He leaves a pile of limp money
on the counter among the many
flat-bottomed birds, but he is unsure
if the carver has seen it.

And as he walks out into a morning
coarse with clouds, he thinks of those
birds—half risen from the water,
half redeemed by the low heavens.

3

"No caribou in this stone," he must
tell him. "Only a sled dog who is sad."
He watches the white man look down
into the premise of dog face, a first eye
bulging. "The stones of the caribou
are more hard to find."

4

For days he keeps his anger to the hills,
mumbling an old Inuit curse
against the chisels of Eskimos,
saying it deep into sleep against
the wagging of tails and the strange howls
of men as lost as their mongrel dogs
out on unending plains of snow.

In one dream the stone is enormous
and the creature that emerges
does not so much rise from the stone
as the stone stands back from him
like a fog moving aside
to let the darkening mountain pass.

5

For days through the window
he has watched the sled dog's patient vigilance,
so that the spring snows have already melted
when he goes to claim what is his.

Alone, the dog waits on the counter
above the granite seals and ivory
sea birds who stay below under glass.
The carver offers the white man a ragged cigarette

and as he smokes he thinks it is,
after all, only a green stone he found once
far up in the blue hills. So he takes it,
puts it in his pocket, and nods to the Eskimo.

And when he walks out into the afternoon,
it parts like water, and he is standing
in an evening thick with lavenders and mauves,
the very colors he is sure he would have chosen.

POOR LITTLE HEART

Bless hers, my mother says,
for the dead man's daughter
whose straight back holds up
the terrible weight of the sanctuary,
whose face takes on the sad colors
of stained glass. And driving home

over Kootenai Ridge, we see a few tall elk
cross the road, slow as old cows.
They let us enter morning, awake
at last. They let the death
we mourned in the valley
drop down deeper.

All day I stir what's in the black
pot. I pare vegetables and toss cores
to the resting garden. Inside us
we carry the gene of death,
our one flaw, which art wants
to make beautiful and so, erase.

The elk head off to their winter
pastures. And bless us to thy service,
my mother says, dipping the ladle.
We sit back among the sinking shadows
and breathe in whatever steam comes up.

GOODNIGHT

Night be good; do not let me die.
— Apache invocation

Evening hangs out its shadows
over the eastern hills. They rise
and flick in the wind. I unbraid
my one braid, unlock its locked crosses,
since it is night,
since whatever is in me of shadow
must also be loosed.

To lie down and dream ourselves
without the lush disguise of flesh
is itself a little of death, a little
less love for our lives.

Night comes on, a steady wind
blowing one way, then another.
Dreaming, our fears go out
and come back,
tossing the dark sheets.
Where have we gone?

Up on the ridge purple thistles
snare a silver thread of starlight
and try, until dawn,
to shake it free.

POETRY FROM ILLINOIS

History Is Your Own Heartbeat
Michael S. Harper (1971)

The Foreclosure
Richard Emil Braun (1972)

The Scrawny Sonnets and
Other Narratives
Robert Bagg (1973)

The Creation Frame
Phyllis Thompson (1973)

To All Appearances: Poems New
and Selected
Josephine Miles (1974)

The Black Hawk Songs
Michael Borich (1975)

Nightmare Begins Responsibility
Michael S. Harper (1975)

The Wichita Poems
Michael Van Walleghen (1975)

Images of Kin: New and
Selected Poems
Michael S. Harper (1977)

Poems of the Two Worlds
Frederick Morgan (1977)

Cumberland Station
Dave Smith (1977)

Tracking
Virginia R. Terris (1977)

Riversongs
Michael Anania (1978)

On Earth as It Is
Dan Masterson (1978)

Coming to Terms
Josephine Miles (1979)

Death Mother and
Other Poems
Frederick Morgan (1979)

Goshawk, Antelope
Dave Smith (1979)

Local Men
James Whitehead (1979)

Searching the Drowned Man
Sydney Lea (1980)

With Akhmatova at the Black Gates
Stephen Berg (1981)

Dream Flights
Dave Smith (1981)

More Trouble with the Obvious
Michael Van Walleghen (1981)

The American Book of the Dead
Jim Barnes (1982)

The Floating Candles
Sydney Lea (1982)

Northbook
Frederick Morgan (1982)

Collected Poems, 1930-83
Josephine Miles (1983)

The River Painter
Emily Grosholz (1984)

Healing Song for the Inner Ear
Michael S. Harper (1984)

The Passion of the Right-Angled Man
T. R. Hummer (1984)

Dear John, Dear Coltrane
Michael S. Harper (1985)

Poems from the Sangamon
John Knoepfle (1985)

Eroding Witness
Nathaniel Mackey (1985)
National Poetry Series

In It
Stephen Berg (1986)

Palladium
Alice Fulton (1986)
National Poetry Series

The Ghosts of Who We Were
Phyllis Thompson (1986)

Moon in a Mason Jar
Robert Wrigley (1986)

Lower-Class Heresy
T. R. Hummer (1987)

Poems: New and Selected
Frederick Morgan (1987)

Cities in Motion
Sylvia Moss (1987)
National Poetry Series

Furnace Harbor: A
Rhapsody of the North Country
Philip D. Church (1988)

The Hand of God
and a Few Bright Flowers
William Olsen (1988)
National Poetry Series

Bad Girl, with Hawk
Nance Van Winckel (1988)